AIN'T LONG 'FORE DAY

New poems

by James Sallis

AIN'T LONG 'FORE DAY

New poems

by James Sallis

AIN'T LONG 'FORE DAY
Copyright©2019 James Sallis
All Rights Reserved
Published by Unsolicited Press
Printed in the United States of America.
First Edition.

All rights reserved. Printed in the United States of America. No part of this book may be used or reproduced in any manner whatsoever without written permission except in the case of brief quotations embodied in critical articles or reviews.

Attention schools and businesses: for discounted copies on large orders, please contact the publisher directly.

For information contact:
Unsolicited Press
Portland, Oregon
www.unsolicitedpress.com
orders@unsolicitedpress.com
619-354-8005

Cover Design: Kathryn Gerhardt
Editor: S.R. Stewart

ISBN: 978-1-950730-99-5

Poems

I.	9
Bright Futures	10
Route 66	11
Paying Respects	12
Reading Poetry at the Local Mexican Restaurant	13
Kindness	14
Mama, Ain't Long 'fore Day	15
Deposition	16
Mother's Day	17
II.	19
Third Person	20
Abundance	21
Free Fall	22
Next Bed Over in ER	23
The Surrealist Works Briefly as a Journalist	24
R.N.	25
Stockholder's Report	26
Silent Night	27
The Departed	28
SHORT STORIES	29
Look Closely	29
Molly So Far from Here	29

Travel   30

III.   31
    Two Moments in America   32
    Dear Interrogator   33
    The Creature's Career Path   34
    Eaves Drop   35
    Forgetfulness   36
    Multiple Choice   38
    What Wednesday Has Packed for Its Trip   39
    Black Rooms   40
    Her Heartbreak   41
    His   41

IV.   43
    A Walk in the Third Year   44
    The Sadness of Saturday Afternoons   45
    Comfort and Ease   46
    Arriving at the Lost City   47
    KINGDOM'S COME   48
    Fleeing the Seen   48
    Contradance   49
    Idyll   50
    The Lessons of History   51
    Adventures in Space-Time   52
    Curb Service   54

V.	55
Sleepless	56
Difficulties of the Day	57
Battlefield	58
Waiting Rooms	59
Self & Co.	60
Daybreak	61
What Became of Our Week	62
Essay	63
It Will All Be All Right	64
The Good News	65
Easements	66
Morning's Resolve	67
About the Author	69
About the Press	69

I.

Bright Futures

When I leave, clouds will not
take over the sky and follow behind you,
so that people to whom you talk
keep watching over your shoulder.

I thought they would.

When I leave, sparrow and dove won't
rush in with crickets or moths
and tunneling worms
and lay them at your feet to console you.

I thought they might.

And I thought that morning light,
the morning after, or the year after, would bring
understanding, two lines of time and memory meet
in a perfect, tidy knot.

But morning light brings only heat
and shadow, day's nest a thatch
of sluffed-off skin, bits of hair,
shabby, unemployable words.

Route 66

I didn't know there would be mountains
until they were lowered into place
and the ground shook,
there at the roadside.

I watched the diner fill
with strangers, how the white van
every day brought new headlines
to the steel box outside.

I sat among them over runny eggs
looking past the high edge of my paper
or the rim of glasses,

laughing at the news, at some pale joke,
at Jessie back in the kitchen playing
Latin rhythms on his pots and pans again,

watching flyspecks on the window
that when you looked long enough became
sedans and pickups and transports and vans
come to take the road somewhere else.

Paying Respects

> "The novel will be at your funeral."
> Norman Mailer

The novel is coming to your funeral.
It doesn't remember you,
but will say it does — all that food
and mock sorrow to feed upon!

Larger than life, insecure,
it will appear in the doorway,
framed in light, and wait
to be noticed. In its mind:
a sweeping cape, a cane
rich with inlay
— behind the jeans and ragged T.

Because time has been repealed,
the novel says, there are problems,
but we can deal
brilliantly with those,
I assure you,

I know what I am doing.

As it grabs a drink
and looks about the room
for interesting behavior,
colorful characters. Everything
is research, even its own breathing.

Reading Poetry at the Local Mexican Restaurant

It should be Lorca, of course.
Neruda. Vicente Huidobro.
But here among booster chairs,
frijoles and policemen, it's not.

Hot, though. And supernally bright.
As I think how I waited on the porch
for you to come back for hours, for days,
imagining that vines would grow over my feet.

Even the postman looked sad.
And rain refused to fall. All I could hear
was traffic outside, like a sea endlessly retreating.

This spill of salsa left behind on page 14.

Kindness

Today I watched a young man
walk with fists clenched
into whatever there was,
which was the morning,
the world,

and nothing more the world could do
than ignore him, out of simple kindness.

Today I watched a hedge
bent like an old woman
over grass and new growth,
but the young wouldn't listen,
nor the old stop talking.

Water in buckets. Sadness of the old,
sadness of the young.

Mama, Ain't Long 'fore Day

My old friend Depression comes by
to tell me no one understands him. He points
to the photo of us in our high school days
that I have on my desk. Good days,
he says, moving around in the chair
trying to get comfortable.

Still alive late in the season,
a mosquito circles and buzzes about him
but doesn't land.

You're on an island, watching life,
looking on, he says.
Whatever once held your life together,
that thread, that filament, is gone.

He pushes himself up
out of the chair to go. Oh – almost forgot:
Loneliness asked me to tell you
she'd be by later to say hello.

Deposition

Along with the year I grow old, forever
out there ahead of myself and pushing
to catch up,

as I must hurry with breakfast now.
They're waiting for me
to testify. The weight of my life
is that of air, they tell me,

yet in what I say, they see
pieces of wreckage suggesting
the beauty and power of the crash.

Mother's Day

I come by the lab to see how
the child you're growing for us
fares.

We walk together out into the greenhouse:
diffuse sunlight, smell of damp and of the dirt
we'll become, orchids closed tight
around their secrets. You've made tea,
which grows cold in the pot.

Remember when we tried to find
a place to eat late at night in Albuquerque?
you ask. We were driving nonstop,
no holds barred, cross country.

Yes -- or that mall in El Paso, bodies parting
left and right as we pushed our way through.
Bells pinged three times, repeatedly,
over the P.A. We never knew why.

Lovingly, proudly, you point to the tendril
just breaking ground, the colorless quilt
of sunlight falling onto it, as we discuss names.

II.

Third Person

He thought for a while he would find an answer
in Paris. There was no one
he knew in Paris. He lived
on back streets, couldn't escape the prejudice of things.

Moments of lucidity, days of disarray. Passions
pulled gently at him. Even as he put out his tongue
to taste it, the world changed.

Abundance

Language being
such a brute thing, he said,
it's a wonder

we survive at all.
Brittle as we are, I mean.

--My philosopher friend, for whom
everything totes a burden
of meaning. One hand

lifts his coffee cup, the other indicates
the umbrella above us,

through which fierce sunlight eases
onto our table top.

Domesticated, he says. Broken, as in
wild horses. Tamed.

What I remember: how that same light
caught in the lens of his eye
as he turned his head,

how children two tables over
stamped their feet, eager for the time
they'd be turned loose.

Free Fall

Unloads it gently, what
she's carried so long.

Feels the weight go away,
the lightness, feels fear
there's nothing to hold her down

now, clouds and wind
and sky, oh my.

How small it is, now
that she looks back.

Wind a voice at her ear
making promises
it will not keep.

Next Bed Over in ER

This is where they cut
to let the world in, she says,
and points with a sturdy finger.

Four-inch stitch like a cat's eye
down her belly.

And here. Here.

Dimple of an old gunshot
like melted plastic rather than skin.
Puckered ridges at a criss-cross —
clean cuts, those.

This one's just a birthmark.
Broke this (holding up her leg)
when I was eight. Did this
with a garden tool.

*Attention: Code red in ICU-5,
Code red, ICU-5.*

This one (she smiles now), this one
is where he said
he couldn't live without me.

The Surrealist Works Briefly as a Journalist

1.

Truth: the old have simply failed to stay young, one of many failures. I meet them most days, those failures, at Bernie's for coffee. Always get stuck with the check, of course.

They all have stories, all but Burt, who sits there quietly. Sometimes when the stories are over, he grunts a bit, or laughs.

Once he lifted his hand at the same moment that, outside, a storm crashed like buckets of sea thrown across the streets.

2.

The Great Poet's eyes are incognito behind the smudges and scratches of his glasses. I'd know that mouth anywhere, the way in performance it turns and twists, but now it's packed away. The Great Poet is silent.

In hope he will speak, I begin sentences and leave them hanging. And so I have found..., I say. The sky today chooses to be...

Dear dear youth, the Great Poet says, as wind comes up behind his voice.

R.N.

Forty years I watched you die
watched you come back

The child they dug out from behind
stacked boxes of china and molded wedding gifts
in the cellar

The old men with no butts
and hairy backs, legs knobbed like fence posts

The girl who excavated her tattoos
and the muscles of her upper arm
with a box cutter

Amy who I worked with
almost twenty years, when

the cleaning woman stopped for a moment
held her mop erect
made the sign of the cross

Stockholder's Report

Madame is in business
with herself. Each morning she consults
the reports, makes sure she retains
controlling interest.

Any moment there could be
a surprise vote, divestments,
disbursements. Lack of confidence
always goes badly.

Today the numbers in the mirror are good.
But another self always stands behind,
watching over Madame's shoulder,
ready to step up.

Silent Night

Words in the end
failed her, as they always do

She lay looking up, trying
to remember

The face hanging there
like a picture in a frame

The frame is wood, filled
with holes

There are worms
inside

The Departed

I always wanted to have
hard eyes, she said. To this day
I'm not sure what she meant.
Times were hard.
It was hard to make decisions.
Day did not yet quite understand
how hard its life would be;
the nights were kind.

Then she was gone, like that word
you know but can't quite get hold of.

So have I lived
with dictionaries and thesaurus
and crossword puzzle books
yet never found it, all these years.

SHORT STORIES

Look Closely

Astonished, I emerge blinking
onto a plain where people stand
whirling their fingers about
like knives.

Sunlight pours over signs
that point off in all
directions, bearing
words like Fate, Home, Relief.

I look up to see one far edge
of a cloud course out quickly like
a lizard's tongue to the sun, and back.

I don't believe the rest of you
have seen this.

Molly So Far from Here

The scholar's weary eyes
lift, and rest
on a young girl's breast.

✻

Her stairs are beached waves. Silent men
ride in on them again and again, bearing
notes, treaties, letters from home.

Travel

My lessons did not cover
this; the phrase book fails.

I can hear them
hauling bodies away.

At 6 AM the night
is a gray feather.

Sky's bright trinkets
won't save us.

III.

Two Moments in America

1.

Each morning I get in my Altima and drive to HangTen where the stories stand around waiting to be picked out for a day's work. Their clothes are shabby and worn. They all look hungry and fit.

Each evening I drive Story back and give him his pay. In the rear view I watch him join the others there on the sidewalk under the sign with missing letters.

2.

Once a man bought a parrot. The parrot had previously belonged to a writer, and would not shut up. Story after story, all day, all night. Did you hear the one about, This woman I know, These three guys were hanging out.

When the man left the cage unlatched, directly alongside an open window, the parrot paused in its current story to remark "I don't think so. No thanks."

When, exasperated, the man grabbed the bird up to throw it against a wall, the parrot said "This is interesting" -- then hurried to finish its story.

Dear Interrogator

Thank you for asking
these questions. I want you to know
that I appreciate your skill,
your professionalism, that
in their wake I've been led to reconsider
many things.

In other lives we might have been friends.
My turn to buy lunch, yours
to pick the restaurant or coffee shop.
I'd tell you about the woman I just met,
how I can't get her out of my mind.

So much begins with what we can't get out of our
        minds.

In some future time, in this better world
you are making,
there will be a day and hour to celebrate
what you and I understand:
that the drum is hollow, made
to be filled with sound.

The Creature's Career Path

It's the monster we love,
always, as if
it has waited all these years for us,
the monster we do our best
to find a name for, so
it will come when called.

At night you read its letters,
the secret messages it leaves
on mirrors, windows, under old t-shirts
you never wear.

We don't know what it eats.
Memory, perhaps. Or weakness.

Or your fear. Perhaps
that is what it needs, your many fears,
gobbling them down one by one
before stepping backward into the dark.

Eaves Drop

    (He says)

The muse whispers, but there's too much noise
to hear. The floors
of the house creak, wind
catches in trees and can't break away.

    (She says)

While moonlight hisses in the cracks.
I know. And who
can choose? When all, like all the misbegotten,
are so beautiful and willing.

Forgetfulness

1.

Because you haven't felt yourself of late
you're sitting in Death's waiting room
watching the office staff twitter and answer phones.

Darkness has thrown itself on your back.
It rides you. In your right ear you hear
the chug of its sugary breath.

2.

Dim in the half-light, it's another wound,
this sky split open: morning
that wants to be full of good cheer,
have a career, a fixed address, benefits.
In his studio across town
Karl stands peering into stone,
teasing the image out
in his mind, olly-olly-ox-in-free.

3.

One day we look around
and the barbarians are gone. They've
gentrified themselves, gone uptown,
bought new clothes, attended community college.
They *matter* now, they vote, they're
people of substance.

4.

We have found another world,
they said, those prodigals, those returnees
one cold September morning, but we cannot find words
to tell how beautiful it is.

They staggered down from the ship, down
narrow ladders onto terra firma.
and fell. Bodies and this world's gravity
had forgot one another.

Multiple Choice

1. This poem begins with
    a. the killing of a spider
    b. a child's birthday party
    c. a female soldier at the front

2. There is
    a. a great deal of physical description
    b. only internal monologue
    c. a loud, crashing storm offstage

3. The people walking around in the poem are
    a. seeking redemption
    b. on tour
    c. searching for the secret of life,
       which they've been told is...
    d. hidden somewhere between the lines

What Wednesday Has Packed for Its Trip

A change of underwear
Its favorite bowtie
Boots and umbrella
Old letters it never got around to reading
Unread copies of The Magic Mountain
A map whose colors have run

Black Rooms

Opium and pipe, the ash
of tobacco, lines on a page –
you follow clues, stepping into them
as one might slippers or shoes too large.

Off balance you lurch toward meaning
and the light, and both elude you.
Proper procedure, intuition –
how to solve the crime that's your life.

Her Heartbreak

Within herself she drifts
to the deep, to water's secret center,
where all pain is done with, forgotten,
where silent dead gather.

Up top, beneath a pale sun,
high-stepping tides persist.
Sailor after sailor is lost.

His

There's an equation to reckon precisely
the rotation of the heart on its axis,
calculate the time it will take loss
to fill these banks.

Alone in the new apartment
he feels the white ceiling pour over him.
A window knocks at the wind.

IV.

A Walk in the Third Year

In the bare branches of elms,
a kind of relief, the safety of hanging things,
of knowing, as I feel my way into this
unadorned day.

*

Words set loose in the mouth,
I pronounce again the old stories, how
choices appear, then close down around us,

so many rifts, so many reefs
we can't sail beyond.

*

Lists accumulate, mailboxes fill.
Wind's idle fingers fumble at the roof.

*

On an evening bright with moonlight
you tell me: Those stories were houses
we built to live in – remember?
Now we rent them out.

The Sadness of Saturday Afternoons

Godzilla is dying.

All Tokyo mourns. London, Chernobyl, Koln, Montova, Alamogordo – they all mourn. Children weep at night and will not be consoled.

From the couch my cat Grace watches, transfixed. Perhaps she believes this tiny being to be edible. Its size onscreen is that of a large bird. It moves.

Or is Grace sad for the beast, for its death? Not knowing that Godzilla will be back, to save again the Tokyo it has destroyed.

Comfort and Ease

1.

Again tonight I will try to hold on to the ghosts,
our ghosts, when they come. I will tell them
what they want to know, if only they will stay --
they who answer to our own secret names,
who might cleanse us of fear and offer up the world
on a chipped white plate with tea.

But as we speak I feel them edging away.
Their eyes go shyly to the room's corners,
to gaps beneath bureau and door, darknesses
where they belong and are safe. They care
that each night we lie here sleep-tossed
and heartbroken, but cannot say it.

2.

In the night as we sleep, soft sounds
come toward us down the hall
as closets empty themselves. Clothes
we haven't worn in years
whisper to one another in drawers.
My shoe by the bed speaks of its aloneness,
though it knows no one listens.

Arriving at the Lost City

There at the butt end of opportunity, doors
slamming shut all around you,
making breakfast for the girls
you spilled oatmeal, a small heap of it
like sand or gravel, something for construction,
beside honey, canned tomatoes, raisins, bread.

Now you turn again and again in your sleep,
as though reaching up with your body, as though
flesh were something you might rise through.

While you lie tossing inside your dreams, your
strangeness, he sprays the kitchen sill
to discourage ants. The clock's hands
move hardly at all;
evening stretches out lazily in the hills.

He thinks he hears you coming back
down the stairs, but it's the wind's shy footfall,
only the wind going on about its business,
making rounds, talking up its wares.

With block and tackle of the past
you reel one another in, into thin air, skin
of your hands sluffing away on the rope.

KINGDOM'S COME

Fleeing the Seen

It's not enough, what I've been given:
this seat at world's edge, the bowl of cereal,
people shouting hello from atop walls,
memories fallen from others's nests.

When the ground gives way beneath you,
as a friend who is no longer with us
used to say, you are falling, yes,
but you are also free.

Why Mercy will not take a meeting
I can't understand. Our people have been
in touch, the table was booked, Mercy's again
a no-show, like Squalor last week.

On the evening news I'll explain once more:
How can excellence be built
with these poor tools you've given me,
these unsatisfactory workmen and warriors?

Contradance

Our friend George no longer speaks
of the Übermensch.
He saw it at work
in the great war and has fallen quiet.
His speeches evaporate like dew.

Is it possible our arts will save us
as we thought
or will they only make us sadder,
as our friend JJ said of big words?

We saw the best minds of our generation
watching Survivor on TV.

Chances are good the sun
will come up again tomorrow.

Remember
not to look into it straight on.

Remember
that you've been warned.

Idyll

In the day of the idiot king
we will all be happy
and great again

This morning I watched angels
alight at a newstand
buy copies and read to one another
laughing

I saw children
vault from their prams
bearing miniaturized assault weapons

Saw the evening sky gloriously alive
with planes
like sharks forever on the move
or they die

O great idiot king it's time
to come and save us
from ourselves, from this burden
of knowledge, these wastes of what might be

The Lessons of History

Tumbleweed just tried to kill Eddie Albert on an old *Outer Limits*. Leapt up, wrapped itself around his face, trembled with power.

Not Eddie! the wallpaper screamed. Not Eddie!

Don't you understand? He's needed at *Green Acres*, further down the line.

Clearly the tumbleweed hasn't thought this through. Though perhaps it's not malevolent, only desperate that there be change, that the old order be overturned.

Adventures in Space-Time

(For Harlan)

The world was so much smaller then, and we
were large. You stalking the podium, four decades
of science fiction's sweet arrogance and bitter self-doubt
on our shoulders, boats we all boldly hoped to put to
        sea
-- if only the sea would take notice. When you walked
behind the podium you disappeared; it was taller than
        you.

Each of us is a nested doll, I whispered, others
the shelters we live inside. Lights flickered in the
        hallway.
All our precious secrets gladly we would have traded
for beans, for a good cup of coffee, for good will or
        reviews.

Two fantasy writers walk into a bar. She would never
        forget
that sweet drop of honeysuckle. The beast and his
        friend
have come to dinner. --The old stories stand around
waiting and wanting to be used again. They purr
and push against our hands. They're hungry.

Here is what they fear: Flop sweat. That we'll discover
their real name. That the lights are too bright,
the audience a blur, and no one laughs at the right time.
That following the map will get them hopelessly lost.

Every month or so you call to say Another one's dead,
Jim, gone into the great silence. Though few enough
listened while they were here. And with them gone, we
     go on
building new worlds, renting those built by others,
fumbling our way towards what it means to be human.

History is two kids crouched under blankets on a rainy
porch reading. History is two adults curled mantis-like
over typewriters as the rain washes their world away.
History is the secret list of those fallen.

Curb Service

The surrealist has opened a coffee shop. His new career!

The mugs bear sketches of sewing machines and umbrellas huddled together on dissecting tables. Men cut in half by windows. Eye-balloons with baskets beneath them. Above the counter floats a giant plaster lobster, leash coiled like a lariat.

Man or woman, the servers wear fuzzy, fur bikinis beneath clear plastic raincoats.

Simply put, it's everywhere in here, dripping from the counter, sticky on table tops, inching across the floor: *Anything can happen.*

It spills out onto the street when the door opens. Children out there reach up and catch the feeling in their hands, keep it in jars as they do fireflies until those small fires go out.

V.

Sleepless

In the wind that is my heart
there are no birds
today. You are gone.

In darkness, dark eyes appear.
This brightness at my back,
alive with memory.

In the night of wolves
a squirrel sits still, trembling
with hope.

Difficulties of the Day

This morning the egg begged me not to plunge it into boiling water. A blueberry leapt from the muffin and tumbled from the counter as I moved it toward the toaster. I gave chase across the floor. The egg sighed as, with a slotted spoon, I lowered it in. The spoon itself asked that I please be quick, it had other appointments.

Battlefield

In the meadow alive
with songbirds, grass tries to remember
what it was like, to live
as a body.

Waiting Rooms

I have cut away all that is self
A successful amputation   I think

Knife in hand   light
through the window   this bloody edge

Pure now

Though only the mortality committee
can be certain

They   will be in touch

Self & Co.

1.

I tried to come back. All roads
were blocked. The last mistake.
They began sending letters,
We'll find you.

2.

Imagine
wind stopped in that tree.

There's enough hurt to go around.

3.

When my arms closed
again, you weren't there,
she said.

No replacement
could be found.

Daybreak

The tree goes on
into sky; branch, leaf, twig
give it no pause.

*

All at once a north
appears
and there's the morning.

*

Lines of the road.
Banks of clouds
filling with sky.

What Became of Our Week

First, birds fell from the sky. Then
we couldn't breathe. All our letters
to congressmen were returned unread.
Long hard days.

———————

Tuesday, Karyn caught me
reading poetry again. Now
she keeps close watch. She knows
what this could mean: scribble scribble,
misdirection, empty hands, waste --

day after day upon which
furtiveness has pitched its tent.

———————

At break of day, all together, the trees
shake off their leaves

which sift to ground and pavement,
silent bells.

Essay

angle of incidence

initiate   celebration   of innocence

the operative   principle   British

co-operation   stress

American   nascent   culture

    kenning

It Will All Be All Right

Frightful necessity enters his eyes
Beside the sun, stranded

As he is beside himself
In distress
Fingers signalling

Does he have hope of stopping
The cloud, the flower
With their terrible hungers

Tumblers roll in the locks
He reaches out, touches with fingers
The unsteady fingers of gloves

The Good News

She knows each day is planet-fall:
unpacking the equipment, setting foot outside
    everything
one does know, sending the message, We made it –
    again.

Is the air breathable?
Are there killer worms? Killer thoughts?
Anyone to talk to?

Checking them off on the clipboard.
Day after day trying to understand
how we'll survive here.

Easements

They were wrong about so much. The price
of freedom. The correct pronunciation
of *Negro* and *epitome*. That in time
I would forget you.

All these years, these mountains
waiting patiently for wind.

And myself up here with them now,
gone small, gone
so gloriously alive.

Morning's Resolve

Eyes fail, looking into the heart
of light, which is also silence.

So very little we can carry, yet must,
in these sad sacks of a human heart.

About the Author

The latest of Jim's 18 novels, *Sarah Jane*, was just published by Soho Press, who are also bringing out a new uniform edition of the six earlier, landmark novels of the Lew Griffin cycle. Other books include three of musicology, a biography of writer Chester Himes, a translation of Raymond Queneau's novel *Saint Glinglin*, and the source novel for the Cannes-winning film Drive. Jim's work appears regularly in anthologies, literary quarterlies, mystery and science fiction magazines, and is translated worldwide. He's won a lifetime achievement award from Bouchercon, the Hammett Award for literary excellence in crime writing, and the Grand Prix de Littérature policière.

About the Press

Unsolicited Press is a small press in Portland, Oregon. The team is made up of volunteers and publishes outstanding fiction, poetry, and creative nonfiction.

Learn more at unsolicitedpress.com

www.ingramcontent.com/pod-product-compliance
Lightning Source LLC
Chambersburg PA
CBHW030131100526
44591CB00009B/609